Victor

FOR BOYS 1990

ALL THIS INSIDE —

Printed and Published in Great Britain by
D. C. THOMSON & CO., LTD.,185 FLEET STREET, LONDON
EC4A2HS. © D. C. THOMSON & CO., LTD., 1989.
ISBN O-85116-445-5

As Alf returned to his welding shop under the railway arches —

BLOOMIN' ADA! HEY, WATCH IT, MATE!

Cor, it's that toffee-nosed Marcus Slade! Don't tell me he was watching the race this afternoon!

Tupper, you might have turned in a better time! Four minutes twenty-one seconds! I ask you! I could have walked it faster!

Is that a fact? Then how come you weren't running, Slade?

A runner of my standing can't be bothered with third rate contests like the Greystone Mile. I'm down for the big one at Melton two weeks from now. I don't suppose you'll be there.

Oh, and why not?

Too many good runners in it for you!

I'll see you there, you toffee-nosed twit! I'll run you!

F 4

But back at his welding shop, Alf was forced to admit that he had real problems.

I've been so busy on that contract for Burman's, I've not had time to put in enough training. There's the phone!

Yes, I know I promised to have your components ready for the twelfth, Mr Burman, and I will . . . Yes, well I'm sorry I was out when you phoned before . . . Just trust me.

Alf was a self-employed welder. He couldn't afford to lose orders.

Looks like overtime for the next ten days at least, but I've just got to get in some more training if I'm to make any sort of showing in the Melton Mile.

Next morning Alf was up at the crack of dawn.

You're an early bird, Alf! Out to catch the worm, are you?

No, Milkie, but I'm planning to run one!

Training early and working till late, Alf completed Burman's contract on time. The day before the Melton Mile he was feeling fit.

I'm good and ready for Marcus Slade now. I'll show that toffee-nosed twit a clean pair of heels tomorrow! There's the phone again! Now what?

I'm sorry it's such short notice, Alf, but we just have to have another gross of S.P.5 components by tomorrow evening!

Tomorrow evening! Look, all right, Mr Burman — leave it with me!

Bloomin' Ada! I'm going to have to work through the night to get a gross of S.P.5's out in time to run in the Melton Mile tomorrow!

And work through the night Alf did!

You're a good 'un, Alf! I really appreciate this. You can be sure I'll be putting more work your way.

TUPPER WELDING DONE HERE

Thanks, Mr Burman. I'll get myself cleaned up now and then I'm off to Melton.

At Melton that afternoon —

Bloomin' Ada, I feel washed out. If there's one thing I like before a race, it's a good night's sleep . . . Heck, I've picked up my old spikes, too, in the rush to get here!

Deep breaths, that's the thing to shake off the cobwebs.

And now for the main event, the Melton Mile.

You made it, then, Tupper? Come to be thrashed, have you?

Alf ran on, biting back the pain, but —

And Slade has done it! He's pipped Tupper on the line! What a fantastic finish!

What did I tell you, Tupper? Oh, come on now — not making excuses, are we?

I never make excuses, Slade.

It gives me great pleasure to present the Melton Trophy to Marcus Slade!

I can't stand the toffee-nosed twit — but he's a darned good miler!

Then two American spectators approached Slade —

Mr Slade, I'm Silas Wakeman of the Florida Athletics Association. This is my colleague, Elmer Spinks.

We have been authorised to invite the winner of the Melton Mile to compete in the Mile of the Masters in Miami — all expenses paid!

A passage has been booked for you on the luxury cruise liner 'Silver Princess' sailing from Southampton in a week's time, Mr Slade. The Mile of the Masters will be run on the twenty-third of next month. Are you interested?

Interested? Gentlemen, I'm on my way!

Ah, Mr Tupper. May we have a word? You had bad luck out there this afternoon.

You noticed? It happens, mate. I ain't complaining.

An admirable attitude to take, Mr Tupper. We need runners of your calibre for the Mile of the Masters.

Unfortunately we are only empowered to pay the expenses of the winner to Miami, Mr Tupper . . .

But if you could get there of your own accord you would be most welcome to take part in the Mile of the Masters.

And run against Slade again? Count me in!

On the way home —

TRAVEL AGENT

Bloomin' Ada! I can't afford all that money — not even with the bonus Mr Burman gave me!

Not to be beaten, Alf travelled down to Southampton where the "Silver Princess" was preparing for sea.

Do you know if there's any jobs going aboard, mate? I ain't fussy. Swabbing the deck — anything, just so long as it gets me to Miami.

Doubt it. You can ask the purser there if you like.

You could be in luck, son. We're short of a hand or two in the galley due to illness. See the head chef, Reg Jenks. Here, you'll need this to get aboard.

Thanks a lot, mate — I mean, sir!

Alf was taken on and shown the ropes. The liner sailed next evening.

Well, get a move on, lad! We've got four hundred hungry passengers waiting for their dinner — and that's only the first sitting!

Give me time to get my sea legs, Chef!

Alf found the work hard and the hours long —

Bloomin' Ada, it's warm down here!

Wait till we're farther south, Alf — then you'll really sizzle!

— but when he was off duty, he still found time to keep in trim.

This is the life! Well, it's all right for some, anyway.

What the blazes . . .! Tupper! What are you doing here?

I'm on my way to win the Mile of the Masters, Slade! Any objections?

9

Come back, dear!

They've thrown in a hurdle or two as well!

I run him! I've won!

Here's to the Mile of the Masters, Slade.

Things will be different then, Tupper! Go peel your potatoes!

When you've quite finished at the Olympics, we've work to do, Tupper!

I gave it all I had there. Darn Tupper! I'll not travel all this way to be beaten by him!

Several days later—

The ship will be docking in Miami in one hour's time, ladies and gentlemen.

So long, fellers. Been nice working with you. This is where I get off.

Good luck in the Mile of the Masters, Alf. Wish we could come and see you, but we're sailing straight on to Nassau.

As Alf waited to disembark—

Are you Alf Tupper? Chef wants you in the galley. He says you've forgotten something.

Forgotten something? Okay, thanks, son.

Before Alf reached the galley—

I'm in the emergency food store, Tupper!

EMERGENCY FOOD STORE

Is that you, Chef? What's up? Don't tell me somebody's been pinching the pickles!

Where are you, Chef? Can't hear yourself speak down here for them fans!

Bye, bye, Tupper!

The door slammed shut.

Hey, what goes on? Let me out of here!

Eighteen hours later —

I've been shouting myself silly down here! Somebody locked me in, and I've a darn good idea who it was — the rat!

Lucky we ran out of currants, Alf. It could have been days before we found you!

Alf saw the Captain.

You've got to turn back, Captain! I've got to be in Miami for the Mile of the Masters tomorrow!

Out of the question. We are bound for Nassau.

Pity you can't hitch a lift on those fishing boats, Tupper. They're heading for Miami.

Alf ran down from the bridge, and on impulse — he jumped!

Tupper, you fool! There are sharks in these waters!

Hold it, mates! Wait for me!

12

ALF's SUPER Puzzles

Hi! lads! It's Alf Tupper calling all you budding sporting brainboxes out there. Have a go at my quizzes and puzzles and see if YOU can be a SUPER PUZZLER. Award yourself one point for every correct answer.

1. TUPPER'S TESTER

CRICKET

1. What material is a cricket ball made from?
2. In which city is the Oval?
3. How many players in a team can take to the field at one time?
4. What are the two pieces of wood that sit on top of the stumps called?
5. What does lbw stand for?

FOOTBALL

1. Who are the Gunners?
2. How far is the penalty spot from the goal line?
3. Which team won the World Cup in 1986?
4. Who was the captain of that team?
5. How many divisions are there in Scotland?

ATHLETICS

1. What country does Ben Johnson come from?
2. Which event does Fatima Whitbread compete in?
3. How long is the marathon?
4. Where are the next Olympics to be held?
5. How many events are in the pentathlon?

TENNIS

1. Who is the youngest ever winner of the Wimbledon men's singles final?
2. How many sets are needed to win a mixed doubles match?
3. Name the famous American tennis venue — Flushing ------.
4. What is the score if it's "deuce"?
5. Which country does Steffi Graf come from? (20)

2. WHO AM I?

Can you figure out who the mystery sportsperson is? There are a couple of clues to help you.

I was born in Australia. My nickname is the name of a dangerous fish. (10)

3. ALF'S BRAINTEASER

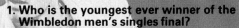

Have a go at this puzzler, but give yourself only ONE MINUTE to work it out. Crikey!

Multiply the number of minutes in a round of boxing by the maximum score with three darts. Divide the result by the number of players in a basketball team. Now divide that number by the amount of holes on a golf course. To that, add the amount of red balls in a snooker match and subtract the amount of points needed to win a table tennis game. What sporting term and bird are you left with? (10)

4. MIXED UP GUYS

Unscramble the letters below to reveal the names of six famous sports personalities. Award yourself two points for every correct answer.

1. YENNK LAGLDISH (FOOTBALL)
2. IMEK SNOTY (BOXING)
3. ANI MOTHBA (CRICKET)
4. EVEST RAMC (ATHLETICS)
5. THEPENS DRYHEN (SNOOKER)
6. EJOS ARAMI ZABALALO (GOLF) (12)

5. SPOT THE DIFFERENCE

At a glance, these two pictures appear to be identical. However, if you look carefully, there are TEN deliberate mistakes in the second picture. Can you find them? (10)

6. WHAT'S YOUR GAME?

These four sportsmen seem to have forgotten what sport they normally play. Can you tell who they are and their usual game? Award yourself two points for each correct answer. (8)

7. DELIBERATE MISTAKE

Study the action pic below and see if you can work out what the deliberate mistake is. (10)

NOW check your answers on the opposite page and see how well you've done.

16

Try your hand at this sports crossword, lads. The answers can be found at the bottom of the page.

(i)

(ii)

(iii)

SPORTS CROSSWORD

What are the initials of these sportsmen?

ACROSS

2. Ex-Celtic player Johnston (2)
5. Similar to bowls, but it's played on ice (7)
6. First blood in a tennis match: ..-love (2) (Number answer)
8. Snooker man Reardon (3)
9. This Moses is the most famous 400 metre hurdler of all time (2)
10. Famous Wimbledon champ of old (4)
12. In darts, the name of the block of wood you throw from (4)
14. See photo (i) (1,1)
15. American football team: .. Rams (1,1)
18. See photo (ii) (1,1)

DOWN

1. The game in America where the final is played at the Super Bowl (8,8)
3. Not an amateur (3)
4. Popular race with a spoon (3)
7. Score for a "bull" in darts (2) (Number answer)
9. Number that lies between 11 and 16 on a dartboard (5)
11. Ex-Liverpool and Spurs goalkeeper. See photo (iii) (1, 1).
13. The current Olympic ice hockey gold medallists (1,1,1,1)
14. Hollow tube passed on in the relay (5)
16. It's worth one point in snooker (3)
17. Liverpool's famous support (3)

ANSWERS

DOWN

1 American Football. 3 Pro. 4 Egg. 7 50. 9 Eight. 11 R.C. 13 U.S.S.R. 14 Baton. 16 Red. 17 Kop.

ACROSS

2 Mo. 5 Curling. 6 15. 8 Ray. 9 Ed. 10 Borg. 12 Oche. 14 B.R. 15 LA. 18 P.E.

SPORTS CROSSWORD

COUNTS!
AT LEAST YOU TRIED AND THAT'S WHAT
ANY SPORTS PROGRAMME?! NEVER MIND,
0-19 BLIMEY! WHEN DID YOU LAST WATCH

LEARN.
SPORT — BUT YOU'VE STILL GOT A LOT TO
20-49 YOU'RE NO MUG WHEN IT COMES TO

SPORT!
YOUR ACT TOGETHER WHEN IT COMES TO
50-59 WELL DONE! YOU'VE CERTAINLY GOT

SUPPER!
YOUR STUFF! AWARD YOURSELF A FISH
60-70 BLOOMIN' ADA! YOU REALLY KNOW

71-80 PURE GENIUS!
you've done.

HOW WELL DID YOU DO?
Now add up your score and see how well

---

5. SPOT THE DIFFERENCE

1. Panel on the door
2. Television leg
3. Footballer on the television
4. Television button
5. Spot on the right foot
6. No turn-up
7. Books on table
8. Lamp flex
9. Shadow on right arm
10. Sole on right foot

6. WHAT'S YOUR GAME?

(i) Ivan Lendl (Tennis)
(ii) Steve Davis (Snooker)
(iii) Sam Torrance (Golf)
(iv) Ian Botham (Cricket)

7. DELIBERATE MISTAKE

There are no lane markings.

---

3. IAN BOTHAM   4. STEVE CRAM
5. STEPHEN HENDRY   6. JOSE MARIA OLAZABAL

---

1. TUPPER'S TESTER

CRICKET

1. Leather
2. London
3. Eleven
4. Balls
5. Leg Before Wicket

FOOTBALL

1. Arsenal
2. Twelve yards
3. Argentina
4. Diego Maradona
5. Three

ATHLETICS

1. Canada
2. Javelin
3. 26 miles 385 yards
4. Barcelona
5. Five

TENNIS

1. Boris Becker
2. Two
3. Meadow
4. 40-40
5. Germany

2. WHO AM I?

Greg Norman (The Great White Shark)

3. ALF'S BRAINTEASER

A duck or zero!

4. MIXED UP GUYS

1. KENNY DALGLISH   2. MIKE TYSON

17

CADMAN

THE FRONT-LINE COWARD

In March, 1918, during World War One, German forces launched a furious attack on the British battlefront in Flanders. Captain Gerald Cadman, V.C. launched himself, as usual, into hasty retreat!

UURGH!

WE'VE NO CHANCE! RUN FOR IT, YOU FOOLS!

The action's hotting up, Corporal. Where's the Captain?

Trying to rally the Company, I suppose. I'd better go and find him.

Only Corporal Tom Smith knew the truth about Cadman . . .

The blighter's the biggest coward in the Army. He's probably found a hidey-hole somewhere.

Gad! What utter rot! I was nowhere near any South Kent positions!

How dare you fellows accuse Captain Cadman, one of the bravest officers in this brigade!

Later . . .

It seems it was young Captain Webber who spread panic among the South Kents. He looks rather like you. Some of the troops identified him at a field dressing station.

Sounds like the wounded officer I brought in, sir. He'd been manning a machine-gun post and . . .

No doubt this Webber chap will get court-martialled for cowardice?

Yes, I expect so. Now I have an important task for an officer made of sterner stuff.

The South Kents' retreat allowed the enemy to capture one of our main stores dumps here at Roubeck. We want you to lead a volunteer platoon back in there to destroy it.

GAD!

And so, that night . . .

Volunteer platoon all ready to go, sir.

Confounded South Kents! Why didn't the Colonel pick one of their own officers?

Because most of their officers are either dead or disgraced by the retreat . . . like Captain Webber who got blamed for what you did.

Deuced insolence, Smith! You can't prove that!

20

I'll give evidence at his court-martial when we get back.

IF you get back! That's a big if for both of us!

In the ruins of Roubeck Town . . .

CHARGE!

Hit 'em while they're looting our lorries, Sarge!

Must make some show of joining in the scrap.

AAAGH!

Gad! I've hit that Hun!

You owe me for saving your bacon, Smith!

Like not giving evidence about Captain Webber's bravery, you mean? Some hopes!

The dump's on the far side of town, sir. Shall we use these lorries?

Well . . . er . . .

Right, Sarge!

21

They made it to the ammunition dump.

22

I see now my mistake. You merely resemble the British officer who fought so bravely to halt our advance yesterday. See, here is an identity bracelet I took from his wrist.

Captain Webber? Holding out at a Vickers gun post?

I meant to return this bracelet with my commendations for such a brave enemy. But if he is not dead . . .

We all soon will be if this dump is blown up too soon!

Get out of here before the whole place goes up!

He's right for once! The lads were a bit quick off the mark in setting off all this ammo!

Move it, Fritz!

Suddenly, a spectacular explosion ripped the air!

HIT THE DIRT!

AAH! MY LEGS!

Huns have blocked our way out with one of our own captured tanks! We're doomed!

How about helping me with Major Fritz here? He's passed out.

To blazes with him!

23

They blasted their way back towards the British lines . . .

Sure beats those lorries we came in on!

And when they got there . . .

We did what we were ordered to do, chum!

Cripes! Lookin' at that sky, you must've blown up the whole of Roubeck!

Next day, at Brigade H.Q. . . . .

Trust you to do more than just your mission, Captain! Not only destroying the dump, but also bringing back this valuable tank and a German Major as prisoner! Well done.

Yes — er — what did that Hun have to say, Colonel?

Quite a lot! Major Von Klug is a talkative chap! Certainly he cleared Captain Webber of any charge of cowardice. He also mentioned his gratitude for being rescued at the ammo dump.

Those South Kent chaps probably made up that report of an unknown officer causing their retreat. Captain Webber will get a medal for gallantry.

So will you-know-who! Don't he always?

The End

25

WHY WEDNESDAY?

HOW SOME TOP CLUBS MADE THEIR NAMES

Have you ever wondered how some famous football clubs got their names? Why Sheffield Wednesday, for instance?

The reason is simple. Over a hundred years ago, the lads of Sheffield who were interested in football and cricket could play only on Wednesday afternoons, early closing day for shop assistants.

In fact, the first "Sheffield Wednesday" was a cricket club. It was in 1867 that a football section began, playing under the same name as their cricketing colleagues.

Cricket also played a major part in the formation of one of the Midlands' most famous clubs, Aston Villa. During the winter months, a bunch of young cricketers from Villa Cross Wesleyan Chapel met regularly for a kick-about in the local Aston park. One day, they decided they should form a proper club and the title they chose was "Aston Villa".

Aside from cricket, there have been many other factors behind the choice of club names.

For instance, take the case of Nottingham Forest. More than a century ago, a great many Nottingham folk played a game called shinney, a form of hockey played with knobbly sticks. Their matches took place on part of Sherwood Forest, made famous by Robin Hood and his band of merry men.

By 1865, the Football League's first member — Notts County — had begun to attract the local sports fans, and the shinney players, in a bid to challenge County, decided to switch sports and take up soccer. To retain something of their past, however, they decided to call themselves Nottingham Forest, and the name has been with them ever since.

Buildings have also played a vital part in the history and formation of club names.

The men who formed the first soccer club in Devon back in 1886 chose the name Argyle Athletic Club, as their first meeting was held in a house in Argyle Terrace, Plymouth. That title was changed seventeen years later to Plymouth Argyle.

Crystal Palace also took their name from a building, this time the two huge glass towers which overlooked the ground on which the F.A. Cup Finals were played from 1895 to 1914. Workers at the Palace started their own football club in the 1870s but it achieved little success and soon folded.

However, a new start was made in 1905. Much has happened since those days. The Crystal Palace was burned down, but by

then the club had found new quarters and today their only link with the all-glass Palace is their name.

Another famous London club whose title comes from their original home is Arsenal. The club was formed way back in 1886 by workers at the huge munitions factory at Woolwich. Their first title was Royal Arsenal F.C., which later was changed to Woolwich Arsenal. In 1913 the Gunners packed up in South East London and restarted at Highbury in North London with the word "Woolwich" dropped from their title.

The story behind the formation of their North London rivals Spurs is also a fascinating one. In 1882, a group of friends held a meeting under a lamp-post in Tottenham High Rd., to discuss the formation of a football team. All were in agreement except for the choice of name for the new club.

Eventually, on the suggestion of one of the lads, they decided to call themselvs Hotspur F.C. Why Hotspur you may ask? It came from the thrilling stories of Henry Percy, son of the Earl of Northumberland, who fought to the death at the battle of Shrewsbury many years before. Percy was nicknamed Harry Hotspur and his family had close connections with the North London district. Three years after the formation, Hotspur became Tottenham Hotspur.

Jimmy's Star Choice

JOHN BARNES

John Barnes' transfer from Watford to Liverpool has proved a magic move for the player and his new club. He's fitted in smoothly to the Liverpool machine, forming a deadly partnership with Peter Beardsley, a partnership that's helped keep Liverpool on the winning way. Searing speed, skilful footwork and devastating finishing make John Barnes a threat to any defence. The fans really start to buzz when John Barnes is on the ball!

ON THE RUN!

Mafia hit man Ricky Scapoli paid a visit to the Calloni family — spitting death!

You mugs die and I collect the loot. But this time the money's all for me!

AARGH!

I've had enough of the Mafia. This is my chance to disappear — and enjoy the good life!

The godfathers will figure these guys got knocked off by the rival Mancini mob. That should leave me in the clear — but I'd better stay low for a while anyway.

HOTEL

CASINO

GAMBLING · POOL

Pays to keep your eyes on the road, mugs!

Later, at a small private airfield.

This five grand is yours if you'll fly me to Mexico —

Sure thing.

But soon after they'd taken off . . .

That chopper . . . is it the police?

I guess not . . .

Mafia mobsters! I'm going down!

Oh, no, you ain't, pal!

Put me down in Mexico or I'll blow you away and fly this kite myself!

Terrified, the pilot flew Scapoli just over the Mexican border.

Tough luck for the pilot! I had to waste him. Now maybe those Calloni hoods will figure I got fried in that kite, too.

A few days later, at Mexico City airport.

I'm being watched! But they won't hit me here. It's too public. The Mafia doesn't like bad publicity.

They're not aboard! No Mafia mobsters ever go where I'm going!

Several hours later, in the small South American republic of Parador.

This is the only place I know where the Mafia won't operate. Presidente Garcia pays them to keep out . . . so's he can rake in money from rich fugitives like me!

Then—

Yes, I know you feel safe here in the capital, Senor Scapoli, but I can make things even safer, by — er — changing your looks.

Plastic surgery face job? Well, you tipped me off about this dump and you've fixed me up good so far, so — yeah, okay!

So, some weeks later, at a private medical clinic.

Great job, Doc! You've even given me a fake scar!

So glad you like your new looks, Senor Scapoli.

My contacts sure fixed me up good! Even down to this jeep. Now to take a look at this small ranch I'm gonna buy.

Some kinda check-point? No sweat, I got papers . . .

Shoot on sight! Open fire!

What the —? AAARGH!

Pedro Diaz, most wanted terrorist in Parador! Even once tried to shoot our Presidente!

Always wears same kind of outfit, drives this sort of vehicle. Looks just like his picture here.

Later that week at a business meeting in Las Vegas.

So our agents in Parador fitted Ricky Scapoli up to look like a local terrorist then tipped off the security police to blow him away.

They recovered what's left of the money he swiped, too.

Never mind the money! The important thing is to let it seem we keep our agreement with President Garcia not to operate in his country. Send extra fees to that doctor and our agents there . . . compliments of Don Luigi Calloni.

The End

TORO

SPACE SAMURAI

It is the Future. Emerging from hyperspace into normal space time was the ship of Toro Tanaka and his crewman Rat. Once an officer of the Imperial Police, the space age samurai had turned outlaw — pledging to fight the oppression of the Terran Empire at every turn.

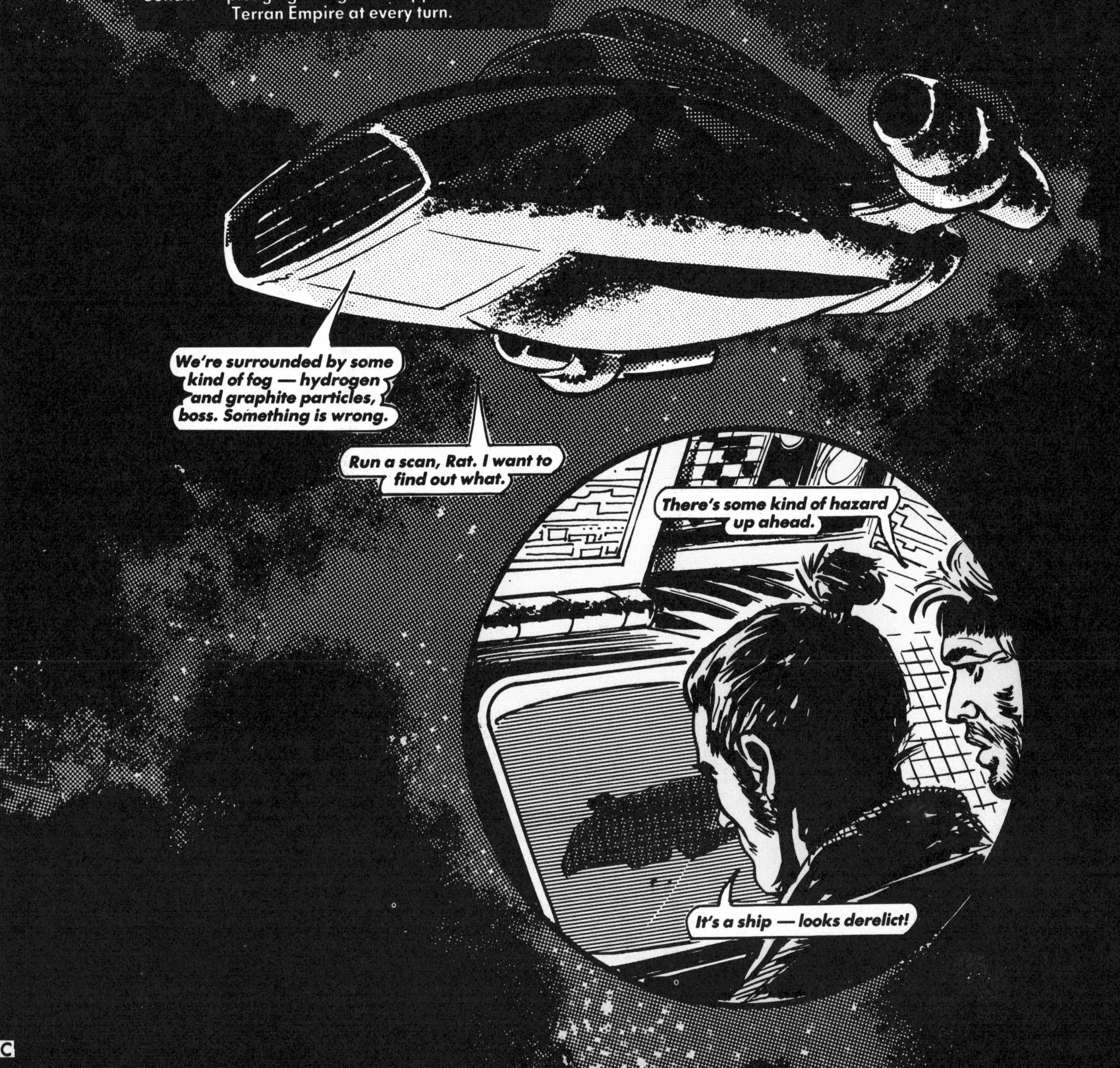

I recognise her — she's the old Devastator! I was on another Imperial ship, the Dynamic, when we tried to hit a nest of pirates on the second planet of Lakheimer's Star . . .

"... only they were waiting with their torpedo shuttles. We took a hammering — the Devastator didn't have a chance!"

An interesting story, Toro, but why should we have broken space fifty light years from Lakheimer's Star anyway? Hey, what's this in the control panel?

ARGHHH!

We've been bugged — and there's only one shifty conniving bunch of eggheads could have done that.

Faculty One! Got it in one —

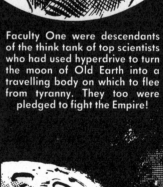

Faculty One were descendants of the think tank of top scientists who had used hyperdrive to turn the moon of Old Earth into a travelling body on which to flee from tyranny. They too were pledged to fight the Empire!

They're somewhere out there — only we can't see 'em because of that light-bending gadget they use to hide their moon.

And my guess is we're going to hear more from them.

Suddenly, from nowhere, a hologram appeared.

Who's that?

I recognise him from police records. He's San Sartos, the old rebel — but he's been dead for years!

Clarinz Harg of Faculty One appeared on the V.D.U. screen . . .

Greetings, Toro. We have been picking up hyperbeam flashes on the police band that report San Sartos as being alive and in hiding on Lakheimer Two! I want you to investigate.

Both images dimmed . . .

If the story is true, the Empire could use his presence as an excuse to hit Lakheimer Two. That must be stopped, so go and play your role of hero!

Hold on, Clarinz. Don't fade out on me.

So we do the dirty work again! It would serve those eggheads right if we just hyperflipped away.

Too late, boss. We got company.

Ignore our warning shot at your peril, stranger.

I am Toro Tanaka, outlaw! I seek sanctuary.

Prepare for boarding and inspection.

There he is — the Lakman. The big boss. They get killed off quick, but they sure live it up while they can!

Toro Tanaka, once Enforcer of Imperial Police, now outlawed and under a death sentence.

I hear you're a top man with a laser blade, Toro — you could be useful.

Unless he is an Imperial spy — a plant with a false background.

It's San Sartos, the old rebel. So he is alive.

There is a way of proving he's with us. He could help me in the taking of the Imperial supply freighter we aim to hit.

Which would just mean risking your rust-bucket and Toro's own ship. I like it.

Yes, I like it.

He likes any chance of me getting wiped out before I can take over his position as Lakman.

Toro's patroller lifted off in company with an old warpshuttle . . .

Boss, ain't grabbing an Imperial supply freighter just a tiny bit unhealthy?

Sartos has a good plan, Rat.

37

Sartos, are you sure that with these co-ordinates, we'll meet the freighter when it emerges from hyperflight?

And so . . .

I have good sources of information, Toro.

Vessels breaking back into space. Sartos was right, boss.

Look at that escort! Two police patrollers with meson turrets.

They are our problem, Rat.

They've spotted us! Now for a game of hide and seek on manual control —

A wide miss. The standard of police shooting has gone down since my day!

So the Sartos plan means us taking on two Imperial ships.

As decoys, Rat — and it is working.

Sartos gave the Imperial freighter an unwelcome message.

Captain, you and your crew will immediately abandon ship or I shall explode it with a meson torpedo.

You leave me no choice . . .

POLICE

The freighter's going into hyperspace. Sartos has done it.

Not Sartos. We have now confirmed that the real San Sartos expired two years ago in a penal colony.

Clarinz Harg appeared as a hologram.

Clarinz! Are you saying we just helped an impostor hijack an Imperial freighter?

More than that, Toro. I fear you have helped some dark Empire scheme. That freighter can now fly into Lak Two without being searched. You must find out what the Empire is up to!

Blister you, Clarinz! Don't fade out on me now.

It's no use, boss. He's gone.

Toro's ship returned to Lakheimer Two.

There's the freighter. Whatever the Empire's up to, I don't expect it to be a mystery for much longer.

Sartos may be a fake, but he's certainly made the pirates happy with this plunder.

Where is he?

You're looking for Sartos? He was heading for the freighter's power-room the last I saw of him.

42

In 1917, during the Great War, a BE-2c two seater aircraft of the Royal Flying Corps, crewed by two Australians and escorted by a British monoplane, attacked a Turkish troop encampment. After dropping its bombs, the biplane ran into trouble.

Cripes! Sandy, we've caught it in the engine!

THE TOSS OF A COIN

Better look for a decent spot to land.

Here comes our Pommie escort now.

Why's Percy pointing like that?

He must be trying to tell us something.

Sandy, one of our bombs has stuck. That's what Percy must have been trying to tell us.

Stone the crows! That's going to make landing a dicey business!

Cross your fingers, Tom. Here we go!

Blimey! I've heard of rough landings but this is ridiculous!

They made it down in one piece — just!

I suggest we get out of here pronto! That bomb could blow any time!

We should be safe here. Look! Percy's landing the Bristol.

When Percy landed . . .

What-ho, chaps! Care for a lift?

Sport, there's no way that tiny kite can carry two passengers.

Get aboard, Tom. At least one of us can be saved.

So you go, Sandy. An old jackaroo like me stands more chance in rough country.

Chaps, perhaps I should mention that a Turk cavalry troop is trotting this way.

Cripes! Let's toss for it.

You call it, Sandy.

Tails!

Tails it is.

Let's make it the best of three.

The Bristol scout took off — with its passenger . . .

Sandy, you won fair and square. Now get going.

Grip tightly, old chap!

Tom, old mate, you never did have any luck at tossing coins. I'd better get out of here. That Turk patrol will be here any second now . . .

Sure enough, as Tom hid out of sight . . .

THE GOALS OF JIMMY GRANT

Spain, France, England and South American aces Umaguay were competing in a four nations contest. Spain, the hosts, clashed with England in the opening game with star striker Jimmy Grant spearheading the England attack.

But Spain struck first . . .

Fendo . . . scores!

Vince Lawlor led the England counter attack.

Chase it, Jimmy!

That's Jimmy Grant! The England danger-man!

D

52

56

England ran out winners.

ENGLAND! ENGLAND! ENGLAND!

The Cup! . . . and the Golden Boot for you!

Nice double, eh? Bit of luck getting that second goal!

Well played, England!

You deserve it . . .

Nice of 'em to clap us off the pitch!

Yeah! Specially since they spent the last hour and a half trying to KICK me off!

But that's football, eh!

The End

Jimmy's Star Choice

CHRIS WOODS

When Chris Woods left Norwich to join Rangers, there were some critics who reckoned it was a downward move for the big keeper. But his displays in the razor-sharp competition of the Scottish Premier Division have proved to the doubters that Chris Woods is a top class keeper. Commanding in the penalty box and able to bring off breath-taking reflex saves, Chris Woods has shown that his career is on the up-and-up.

THE FUGITIVES' CLUB

The Fugitives' Club had been set up after the Second World War by men of all ranks and services who had escaped from enemy prisoner-of-war camps. It had grown dry and stuffy over the years, but tonight was a special occasion — the club had a new member!

Can't just sit there, old boy! You have to tell us a story. It's part of being made a new member.

We haven't had a new member since the Korean War!

I'll tell you a story, but I'm mentioning no names just yet. I'm calling the characters Corporal and Private for the time being. Their escape was planned in 1943 . . .

Everything had been prepared . . .

You've been told how to reach the first safe-house. The next one will be given to you there for security reasons. Good luck, both of you.

"They made the break the following night. It went well — too well, I suppose . . ."

How the blazes did they manage to keep the guards off this stretch for so long?

Bribery I suppose — I dunno. Just get on with it, Corp!

Soon—

What are you doing, Corp? You'll get your feet soaking wet — and it's freezing!

They'll use dogs, idiot! This should fool 'em for a while.

And, at the first safe-house on the line.

After some rest, you will find two bicycles in the back shed. Leave at dawn and join the factory workers as far as the main cross-roads. Then . . .

At the next safe-house—

But — won't the local people know we're not the usual dustmen?

No problem. The round's been done. You're just taking the rubbish to the big tip out of town. You'll be met there.

They must be the blokes who are meeting us. But why so many?

They soon found out!

One of you is a German plant. If we can't find out which, then both of you die!

Eh?

So — so that was it!

Suddenly, the Corporal snatched a gun from the nearest man, and—

That torch! You've been signalling to the enemy! I knew something was up. You STINKING, NAZI SPY!

Here! I took it away from him — but not in time, obviously.

Well done, my friend. We must get you across the Channel to safety. A boat is waiting.

So! Since the Private died, you must be the Corporal, my friend. An exciting tale.

Oh, no! I was not the Corporal . . .

The Corporal, because of an old wound, was discharged. He got a job at a munitions factory, and some time later the munitions factory was blown to smithereens in a raid. It happened to be his night off duty . . . The next job he got was at an aircraft factory. That also received a direct hit . . .

So — so the Corporal was the real spy! The other man was innocent! But if the Private was killed and you are not the Corporal—

I was the Private. That bullet didn't kill me . . .

But it took away my memory. All I knew was that I was British and on the run. I was given cover by a French farmer. Five years ago my memory returned, and I have spent the rest of the time hunting down that Corporal . . .

He was never caught. After the war he stayed on, retaining his cover as a war hero. But I have found him, and now I seek revenge and justice . . .

He — he has a gun!

Looks like a heart attack! Someone call an ambulance!

N-no! You — you died! I — I killed you! You — ARRGH!

Too late! He's dead.

Good grief man! Would — would you have used that thing?

No. It wasn't loaded. I was just going to scare him and then hand him over to the authorities.

He thought he was safe. He was sure I was dead. But in the end, justice was done. The past caught up with him just when his heart was old and weak . . .

THE END

Deep in the jungle of Borneo, a lone strongman did some weight training. He was Morgyn the Mighty — the strongest man in the world!

MORGYN THE MIGHTY

Enough of this. I have promised to visit my Dyak friends. Their village is nearby.

But Morgyn was in for a shock . . .

The village is deserted. Where are all the people?

Even my friend Doctor Jogjal is gone, his clinic abandoned like the native longhuts.

There should be many tracks if all those people moved on — but there are none!

Suddenly, a net appeared from nowhere . . .

UURGH!

65

E

Monkeys! But it's impossible!

BUT NO NET CAN IMPRISON MORGYN THE MIGHTY!

They're running off, but they're the first monkeys I ever knew who could use a net like that!

Smoke! It's from that other village I passed through. I'd better get over there.

Morgyn ran, until . . .

There it is. One of the longhuts is on fire! But this village is certainly not deserted!

The men are being rounded up like cattle!

But it seems one of them is fighting back!

The villager didn't stand a chance!

UURGH!

AIEE!

These people are evil! One touch of that stick and the villager was out cold!

Suddenly there was a blinding light!

AHHHH!

Everybody — everything — is gone . . . just like Doc Jogjal's village!

Except the raider killed by the villager . . . and what's this? Swamp mud on his legs!

Morgyn travelled . . .

There's a lot of swamp around here, but I know only one place where ferric oxide forms a good part of the mud mix.

67

Crocodile! And he's not looking too friendly!

Must try not to harm an endangered species.

Morgyn, my apologies for the spot of trouble, but the reptile is conditioned to attack all who come this way.

Doctor Jogjal! Where did you spring from? Are you all right?

Never have I been better, Morgyn — as will be the case with you when you serve the Traveller.

What Traveller? UURGH!

Just the Traveller, Morgyn.

The glare dimmed and suddenly the surroundings were different.

This village is new to me.

It is home for the helpers. The Traveller allows them comfort during their short lives.

They are primitives of limited ability, but with their own small importance in the great plan. Of course, our superior education make us even more useful.

Can this be my friend Jogjal talking?

These are the new helpers you saw being enlisted. Observe their happiness in their new life.

They look like zombies — just like all the others I see here.

Now come with me, Morgyn, and do not be alarmed. We are entering the airlock of the outer portal.

This is the vessel of the Traveller. It carries him faster than light across the sky.

A spaceship!

Yes, Morgyn, this ship has carried me across space and time from a world not unlike this earth.

" . . . though perhaps more humid and richer in oxygen"

These differences make your planet uncomfortable for my kind, but they will be eliminated by tapping the magma gases deep under the Earth's crust — changes which the labour of primitives like yourself can help bring about.

Do you really believe I would help in the taking over of my world by aliens?

Yes, Morgyn, you will help. You will be happy to help.

AHHHHH!

I SHALL HELP. THE TRAVELLER MUST BE HELPED.

Morgyn walked off in a deep trance.

What must be done is in your minds.

We understand and obey.

This group of elderly natives is unfit for work — but the Traveller has a use for them.

Go through the airlock into the ship.

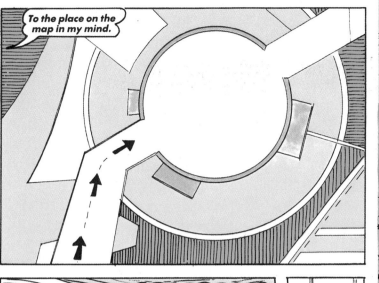

To the place on the map in my mind.

This way for you. You can yet serve the Traveller. You will make useful protein.

Protein! People as food! It is monstrous!

"Not at all. How else could they help my own people after their long journey through the stars?"

What point is there in preparing this planet if my people do not survive to become colonists?

So my people help you by becoming food.

NO! NO!

You foolish man, Morgyn.

STOP! URHH!

71

Now you too must become nutrition for the people of the Traveller.

Must be some kind of neuron jammer he used! Hits the nerve centres . . . got to fight it!

THE TRAVELLER MUST BE STOPPED!

Sorry, but I must make sure you have a nap, Jogjal my friend.

Morgyn, you disobey me. Now you shall know the physical discord you term pain.

ARGH!

Pain can be countered by pain. It is my only chance.

I cannot be overcome!

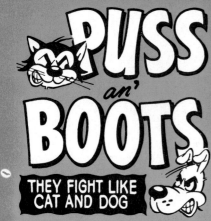

78

79

STRONGHOLD

In the last months of World War Two, German mountain troops launched a furious assault on a castle known as Schloss Eigler in their own Bavarian Alps.

Keep firing! Wipe out that nest of traitors!

Enough! We cannot hold out against this attack!

So do we now surrender, Count Otto?

To be shot or hanged by the Nazi scum? Never, Hans!

F

Leave that machine-gun to fire on fixed lines while we make our escape.

Not even we know all the secret passages under the castle.

Ah, but I do. It was my ancestors who made them.

It grieves me to leave our Von Eigler family home to be fouled by Nazi swine but our fight here is over. We must slip away through the forests.

A week later, at an Allied Army H.Q.

Von Eigler has given us the information we need to get men into his castle. We can trust him. For years he has organised secret anti-Nazi resistance groups.

His castle commands the main mountain road into Bavaria. He hoped to turn it into a stronghold to aid our advancing forces . . . and to resist Nazi SS troops who may be planning to make a stand in that district.

Later, at a nearby airfield.

Here are Count Otto's plans of his castle, Major Brett. Get in there, then hit the Germans hard!

We'll do our best, sir.

That night.

Achtung! Enemy aircraft!

82

Move it! That light may have spotted us dropping in.

Rifle shot!

Just to catch your attention, Major Brett.

How'd you know my name? Who the blazes are you?

Major Steiner, Special Intelligence. I was dropped in a few hours ago.

He looks and sounds like a Hun!

Perhaps because I am part-German. Before you let your Sergeant Maxon shoot me, Brett, I also know that your mission here is codenamed "Stronghold".

Some minutes later.

We must cross this road to reach Schloss Eigler.

Why here . . . with Waffen SS troops on guard?

They patrol the whole road. Better take them by surprise than let them take you.

Achtung!

83

HIT THEM HARD!

AAARGH!

Nein! AAAGH!

We cannot risk leaving any wounded here.

Still got doubts about him, Max?

Why not, Major? Rats often kill their own kind . . .

One of the entrances to the castle is behind a ledge hidden by a pinnacle up here.

I know that from studying Count Otto's plans.

So why do we need you, Steiner?

You don't. You can carry on without me now.

84

Proper maze of tunnels!

We'd be lost without these plans.

The Count kept a well-stocked cellar!

Ammo and explosives, bedding and food rations!

During the next few days and nights . . .

. . . Brett and his men . . .

. . . carried out attacks on the Germans . . .

. . . causing mayhem and devastation . . .

Poor old Jerries! Foot-slogging out again to search for us!

While we hide out smack under their cosy castle barracks!

85

So far our targets have been SS troops and stores. Now we must make sure this place can't be used as part of their stronghold.

So we blow up the castle! I get you.

Odd how we never met up with that Steiner bloke again.

Must have had other jobs to do. No SS thugs in the castle. Just ordinary mountain troops. So I'll go out under a white flag to warn the garrison commander . . .

Suddenly . . .

No need, Brett! I have already warned them.

STEINER!

Shoot the Hun rat!

Too late for that, Sergeant!

Get moving, lads! Fight your way out!

No chance! Stand still!

So Max was right! You ARE an enemy!

Depends what you mean by enemy. I have let you hit SS troops hard. But before the war I was an officer in this Ninety-Third Jaeger Regiment.

From a window overlooking the castle courtyard.

Their battalion Colonel and two company commanders have been arrested by the SS and charged with anti-Nazi plots. Now these Jaegers are mustering to attack the SS H.Q. in Stromberg town.

So?

So the SS may expect them. They could get slaughtered. So such an attack is better done by a small group of special raiders.

You mean us? You want us to go rescue three Hun officers?

Either that or the Jaegers will imprison you all in the castle dungeons. Then Heaven help you when the SS take over here.

That evening.

I don't feel right taking orders from that Hun spy!

We've little choice, Max.

Can't be helped if we're to keep that castle out of SS hands. Those SS panzers may be watching out for a mob of angry mountain troops, so let's sound like them.

Halt! Where are you going?

None of your business! So get knotted, SS cops!

Get yourselves ready for the attack!

Himmel! What are you . . .?

Out of my way, Fritz!

UNNGH!

Eliminate this lot! Get the prisoners out!

EEAAAGH!

Minutes later.

Are we rescued from the SS only to be captured by the British?

Not exactly, Colonel Von Brandt.

Back at the castle.

Hurrah for our Oberst Von Brandt!

He seems popular with his men.

Good to meet you again, Hauptmann Steiner!

How can he be a Captain in the Hun Army and a Major in British Intelligence?

88

So in return for rescuing me and my officers you expect my Jaegers to defend this castle against SS occupation?

That was the idea, Colonel.

A foolish idea! I will not have my men slaughtered! By dawn they will be disbanded and dispersed in the forests.

But Steiner promised . . .

I promised nothing. At least now you can have your castle stronghold all to yourselves.

Just after dawn.

Best part of an SS Panzer Division approaching!

All the Jaegers have left us are a couple of mountain guns! I'll have a look for any explosive charges lying around.

Meanwhile . . .

Not a thing — but without explosives we've no chance!

Calling Panzer SS Kommandatur. I will direct attack . . .

You'll direct nothing, Steiner!

Yes, I also hold rank in the SS as Sturmfuhrer Steiner. But before you shoot me, Brett, take another look outside.

All I see is a huge attacking force.

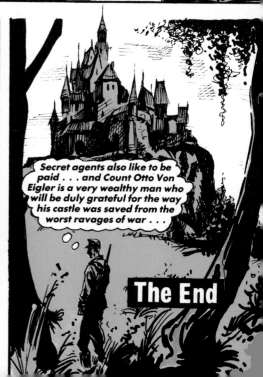

The End

Jimmy's Star Choice

STEPHEN HENDRY

He's one of the youngest players in top flight snooker, but already Stephen Hendry is seen as the most likely successor to Steve Davis as snooker's number one.
An ice cool temperament and deadly potting skills have enabled young Stephen to take the snooker world by storm in the past couple of years. Already he has several major titles to his credit — now his sights are set on becoming the new king of snooker!

LAST CHANCE

Jack Last was an ex-pupil of the Galley Trust, a school that prepared orphan boys for a sea-going trade.

Afternoon, Captain Last. Berthed for long this time?

Only till the evening tide. Then I'm away with grain on another down-coast run.

Wakey-wakey! Where'd you get that tie?

It's mine . . . I was given it when I left orphan school.

The impudence of the layabout!

Matey, come along with me. An old Galley Slave, eh! Well so am I!

Small world, ain't it? I don't mind coming if you got some grub in mind.

. . . with an extra member.

Get them spuds boiling, then you can scrape rust in the chain locker.

Maybe I should have stayed on shore.

That night . . .

It's the Greek. Flash the signal.

He's answering. The stuff's going over.

There it is.

Why are we stopped?

None of your business, Tommo. Get back below!

A tenner. Is that all?

With clothes and food it's more than you're worth, lad. Now sling your hook.

Next morning, the Last Chance off-loaded her cargo.

Some free advice from a fellow orphan, Tommo. It's never too late to make something of yourself.

I'll remember that, Captain Jack Last.

Later . . .

He's expecting you, Captain.

A full tally, Jack — twenty packages fished out of the grain. I'm still not happy we're running drugs.

Drugs are where the money is, partner. A few more trips and we'll be set for life.

Suddenly . . .

The yard's swimming with cops and customs.

Keep 'em busy while I get out the back way.

Just as well I keep my motor parked in the lane.

Tommo. What are you doing here?

Just waiting for you, Captain.

I knew you'd be needing your posh car.

What . . .

HEAD-HUNTER Of The GALAXY

Bo Rogan was a bounty-hunter in the 22nd Century. In his space-ship he roamed the universe, tracking down criminals with a price on their heads.

BO ROGAN

When Rogan called in at the Integral Bank one morning, he found someone making an unauthorised withdrawal—

ARRRGH!

SAFETY DEPOSIT

Out of my way — or SHE dies too!

What the —! That lunatic isn't even masked!

From this angle I can take him!

But—

Look! Another one — must be an accomplice!

TAKE HIM!

Let me go, you idiots!

Get off me! The real hood is getting away!

UNGH!

By the time Rogan had freed himself—

It's pointless going after him. He'll be lost in the city crowds. Someone call an ambulance and the L.E.G. men.

Poor Mister Masters — he's hurt — maybe dead . . .

Later, when Chief Inspector Foley and the men of the Law Enforcement Group arrived—

Just what was this Mister Masters' job, lady?

He took depositors into this safety-deposit vault. Only he could open the boxes. He took that — that terrible man down here . . .

I can identify him, Foley. I—

Who needs you, Rogan? There are plenty of witnesses PLUS the bank video which will have filmed the whole thing. Get lost! I don't like the smell of bounty hunters!

When Rogan had left—

This guy Masters isn't dead, Foley. He's in some kind of trance.

Get him down to HQ. Bring him out of it. He'll tell us why he took that hood down into the vault in the first place. Must've known him!

98

Later, at the Law Enforcement Group Headquarters—

Masters was in a hypnotic trance. The bank-robber had mesmerised him — forced him to take him down and open the boxes. But the woman saw something odd going on and screamed. That blew the whole thing. But the robber still got away with a tidy sum in jewellery and other valuables.

Then we'll soon have him!

That explains why the hood didn't wear a disguise. He was over-confident — expected his plan to work. But it went wrong and all we have to do is feed what we know into the Central Computer and we can pick him up. This time WE get there first and not Rogan!

But Rogan wasn't idle. He was using Chris — his Cross-Reference Information System — to patch into the Central Computer.

Okay, Chris, baby! Foley will be using the Central Computer to knit-up what he knows. Let's eavesdrop . . .

But in a city hideout not far away—

Now I'll be identified and a block will be put on all terminals. I'm trapped — unless . . .

While Rogan was checking over the visual display on Chris—

A visitor approaching, Mister Rogan. Advisable to clear the screen.

Okay, Chris. Activate recording procedure for the visitor!

You! The bank robber!

Relax, Rogan. Just look at me. Listen to me.

Within seconds Rogan was under the man's hypnotic influence.

I know you have your own space-craft, Rogan. It is at the private space port just outside town. You will do just as I ask you and take me there. You will then fly me to the destination of my choice . . .

I shall do as you wish . . .

99

Foley had identified the bank robber as Magil Perlakk, an ex-psychiatrist disbarred for illegal practice. They went straight to his last-known address—

Okay, Perlakk!

Too late, sir — he's flown the coop!

Look, sir! Rogan's name has been circled in the directory!

ROGAN! So THAT'S how he happened to be at the bank just at that moment! Oh, man, am I going to enjoy THIS snatch!

Rogan was already in his craft at the space port.

Computer-terminal transfer initiated, Mister Rogan . . .

Couldn't have been smoother, Rogan. Your pass took us straight past the gate without question. Now you'll take the following course . . .

That Bo Rogan's craft taking off?

Yes, sir! Any problem?

Not if I can help it, laddie! Get me in touch with Sub Orbital Perimeter Patrol — NOW! And have a craft ready for me five minutes ago! GOT IT?

Y-yes, sir!

Sub-Orbital Perimeter Patrol trying to make contact. Demanding return to space port . . .

Blast them out of the sky, Rogan!

. . . you will sleep. It must have been a trying time for you.

And while you sleep, Rogan, time will be ticking by . . .

I must allow enough time to get well clear. The explosion from this bomb will be enormous!

Meanwhile, Foley was in pursuit.

Almost lost Rogan's bleep. Looks like he's moved into L Phase Hyperspace and is heading for Barsalon.

Are you hearing this, LEG 8 and 9? There's an Inter-Galactic Space Terminal on Barsalon. We lose Perlakk and Rogan there and we can say goodbye to 'em! MOVE IT!

On Barsalon—

Farewell, Rogan! You've been of great use to me, but you'll never wake up again!

On board Rogan's craft—

Mister Rogan. You are ignoring the X.R. Alert. There is unexplained electronic activity and explosive material unregistered in my inventory banks . . . I am about to initiate ORSOC since I regard this as an emergency . . .

ALERT! UNREGISTERED MATERIAL

ORSOC (Operator Restrainer Seat On Contact) was an anti-theft device. It pinned a thief to the seat and gave him a mild electric shock.

Aaaargh!

Forgive me, Mister Rogan, but I HAD to snap you out of it somehow! Now I'll release you.

105

PANTHER'S PREY

Joe Bell and Tom 'Timid' Timms were good friends all their lives. It all started in 1930 when they were eleven-year-old new boys at senior school, and Tom was picked on by the school bully . . .

Get up, Timid! I've got punches you haven't even seen yet!

Come on, Timms. That's the fourth time he's knocked you down.

That's enough! How about you trying another new boy — me?

For cheek, Bell, I'm going to give you what I just gave Timms!

Cor! Never seen Bloggs beaten yet. Doubt he'll be bothering Timms again!

A few days later —

My uncle gave me two tickets for the circus. Would you like to come?

Great stuff! Can't beat a circus for excitement.

But outside the circus —

RUN FOR YOUR LIVES! THERE'S A PANTHER LOOSE!

Tom's tripped! And that big cat is heading right for him!

108

I can't get up and run. I'm scared stiff!

I have to get that brute's attention away from Tom or he's had it!

It didn't like that. I'll give it another one!

RUN, JOE! IT'S COMING FOR YOU NOW!

BACK, SHEBA!

She hates blanks being fired, boss. Scares her rigid!

Seconds later the panther was netted, then returned to her cage.

That was a brave thing to do, lad, drawing that cat away from your chum.

I had to. He owes me a quid!

Time passed, and both Tom and Joe joined the Army when war broke out in 1939.

That's the last film I see before I go off to camp. I doubt if there will be time for much pleasure when I start square bashing.

Pity we'll be so far apart. I'm posted right down South.

The pals' wars took very different paths . . .

Come on, lads. Let's flush the blighters out!

What a life. Doing everything in triplicate all day. I'm a real chairborne warrior!

109

In 1945, after the Allies had crossed the Rhine —

Hey! Blow me if it isn't old Timmy asking directions from the M.P.!

I'm really lost. I've these typewriters to deliver and I'm miles from where I should be.

I'll show you the way to H.Q. I'm heading that way.

Joe! Fancy running into you! Get into the front beside me.

At that moment at the German headquarters —

Gentlemen, we shall counter-attack all along their line. With this surprise we shall hurl them back across the Rhine!

Once more we shall taste victory, Herr General.

In thirty seconds our massed batteries will open up. This will shake them!

The Allies WERE shaken by the bombardment. Then the German armour and infantry moved up —

Like the old days, eh, Brandt? Takes me back to Poland and France.

Ja! Good to be once more on the offensive!

Hastily the British regrouped —

The Jerries caught us napping. Split whole units. But as from now we are a battle group and can still hurt them.

Bunch of odds and sods, more like. Cooks, clerks and confused clots!

Tom and Joe ran into trouble —

Heck! Where did that come from?

110

RUNNING the GAUNTLET

During Napoleon's campaign in Prussia in 1806, a battery of French artillery held off a determined counter-attack by the enemy. But they were running short of ammunition—

Major, the wagon lines are trying to send up more ammunition.

It is needed if we are to keep up this rate of fire much longer.

But then—

At the wagon lines.

Boys, that last try at supplying the guns did not go too well. To spare myself a rush of volunteers, I intend to let the bones decide who goes next.

113

Each man threw the dice.

Two sixes! Brissot, nobody is going to beat that, but we'll give the other lads a chance just to be fair.

Another winner came up.

Young Laclos and Brissot! We could have a throw-off, but why should one be disappointed? I accept both gallant lads as volunteers to run the gauntlet!

Stick close to me, Laclos. I'll take care of you, boy.

Thanks, Brissot.

The wagon mules were whipped up.

YEE-AHH!

The Prussians have spotted us. It'll be hot work from here on, Laclos.

Be ready to cut loose any mule that goes down.

Nearly there, boy. We're going to make it.

OOOOOOH!

Oh, no!

Then just on half time.

NOOOOO!

At half-time . . .

Sorry, Boss.

Don't worry, son. You were in the right place both times. Your positional play is first class. Keep it up. The goals will come.

Second half . . .

The boss has got faith in me! I've got to prove him right!

I made it!

YE-E-SSSSS!

I was right, Ernie.

About what, Boss?

There it goes. Now to deal with those mules.

Major, he has got through!

Splendid fellow! Just when we are down to our last few rounds.

At dusk, Brissot staggered into the wagon lines.

Had my skull clipped by a chunk of case-shot. Knocked me clean off the wagon or I'd have been blown up with poor Laclos.

But Laclos lives! He took that wagon to the guns.

It's Laclos! He's coming in!

I had better go greet the returning hero.

It should be me coming in to the cheers of my mates. Who knows what lies that pup is going to tell about old Brissot.

BRAVO, YOUNG LACLOS!

The End

One is capable of bulleting along a motorway at 150 mph, the other leaves every other passenger plane in the world in its wake as it rips across the sky — but both the Sierra Sapphire RS Cosworth and Concorde have this in common. They're packed with all the glamour and power of

SPEE

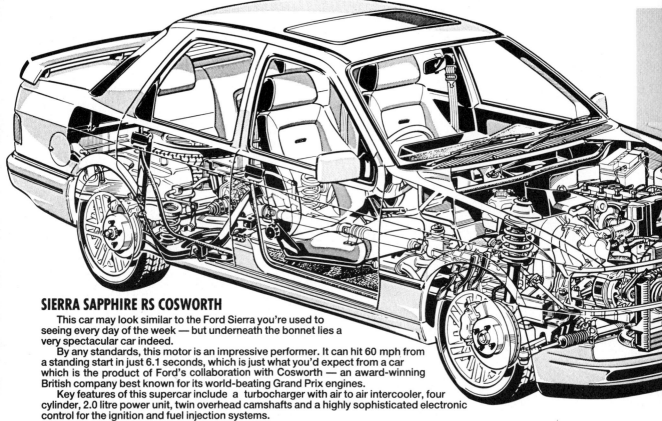

SIERRA SAPPHIRE RS COSWORTH

This car may look similar to the Ford Sierra you're used to seeing every day of the week — but underneath the bonnet lies a very spectacular car indeed.

By any standards, this motor is an impressive performer. It can hit 60 mph from a standing start in just 6.1 seconds, which is just what you'd expect from a car which is the product of Ford's collaboration with Cosworth — an award-winning British company best known for its world-beating Grand Prix engines.

Key features of this supercar include a turbocharger with air to air intercooler, four cylinder, 2.0 litre power unit, twin overhead camshafts and a highly sophisticated electronic control for the ignition and fuel injection systems.

And the Cosworth has got the looks to match, with its distinctive Sierra shape allied to wide-rim alloy wheels and ultra-low profile Dunlop sports tyres. Every inch a Speed King!

ED KINGS

CONCORDE

Concorde is a dream that came true.

Although it has never been the commercial success the British and French hoped it would be when it first entered service over ten years ago, the plane is as technically thrilling today as it was to its designers when it was still on the drawing board in the early sixties.

With its distinctive delta shape and unique hinged nose it beats any other Speed King of the air for looks, while the tremendous power of its four Olympus engines develop an astonishing 35,000 lbs. thrust at take off and can hurtle the plane through the air at 1450 mph — that's more than twice the speed of sound!

Travelling in Concorde is still the ultimate in air transport!

ALF and JIMMY'S LAFF-IN

Stop here for some great laughs, lads!

Yes, we've put together some of our favourite jokes. Enjoy yourselves.

YOU MUST BE REALLY POPULAR AS A REFEREE. THE FANS HAVE SENT YOU ALL THESE GIFTS!

She stood on the bridge at midnight,
Her lips were all a quiver.
She gave a cough,
Her wig fell off,
And floated down the river!

What did the orange squash say to the water?

ANSWER: Diluted to meet you.

How many balls of string would it take to reach the Moon?

ANSWER: Just one huge one.

What do you get if you cross a sheep with six radiators?

ANSWER: Central bleating.

What do you get if you drop a piano on an Army camp?

ANSWER: A flat major.

NOW I REMEMBER — I WAS SUPPOSED TO JUMP OVER THIS!

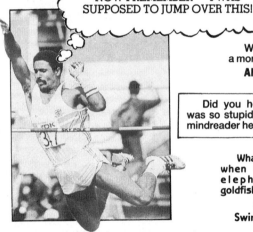

What do you get if you cross a monkey with a flower?
ANSWER: A chimp-pansy!

Did you hear about the boy who was so stupid that when he went to a mindreader he got his money back?

What do you get when you cross an elephant with a goldfish?
ANSWER: Swimming trunks!

CAN I SHARE YOUR SLEDGE?

WE'LL GO HALVES. I'LL HAVE IT DOWNHILL, YOU CAN HAVE IT UPHILL!

FOOTBALL FUNNIES

YOWP! THE PITCH IS AWFUL ICY TODAY!

SLIP

HOW ON EARTH ARE THE OTHER TEAM KEEPING THEIR FEET SO WELL?

SLIDE

I THINK THE CHOICE OF STUDS PLAYED A BIG PART IN OUR VICTORY TODAY! HA-HA!

120

Hit it, Sammy!

OHHHHH!

Sammy Todd's goal-scoring touch with Third Division Barton Athletic had earned him the nickname "Super Sammy". When Lester Jack, manager of First Division Brentwood City signed Sammy for close on a million pounds, great things were expected of the striker. But . . .

SUPER SAMMY

In five games, Sammy had failed to find the net — and Lester Jack was not pleased!

You great useless object! Two open goals and a missed penalty! What's the matter with you, lad?

Sorry, Boss. I guess it just wasn't my day.

Wasn't your day? A chimpanzee with a wooden leg could have stuck that last one away! I'm warning you, lad. Get me some goals on Saturday — or else!

That ball was greasy this afternoon, Boss. It took some controlling.

City's next game was against league leaders Granton United —

I want no excuses, lad! You've got ninety minutes left to prove I wasn't out of my mind when I signed you! Got it?

Got it, Boss.

It doesn't make sense, Sammy. You were cracking 'em in from all angles with Athletic. What's gone wrong?

I wish I knew, Charlie. When Lester Jack signed me I thought, this is it. Division One — next stop the England team. Some hopes now!

Among the crowd was Pete Ross, manager of neighbouring First Division Brentwood Rovers.

Come on, City, let's have one!

A chance for Sammy soon after kick off.

Put it away, Sammy!

He's muffed it!

Go for it, Sammy!

By half-time, United had taken a one goal lead. Then early in the second half . . .

Sammy held back! He was in a perfect position to put that one away!

I reckon he's got so scared of missing he's afraid to have a go!

Then in the last minute . . .

Yours, Sammy!

OOOOOH!

You might well hang your head, lad! That does it! I'm going to make you sorry you ever kicked a ball . . . !

Easy, Boss. Watch your blood-pressure!

Then in mid week, Brentwood Rovers made a shock offer for Sammy.

A deal, Lester?

He's all yours, Pete! And the best of luck!

TODD DROPPED

NOT GOOD ENOUGH FOR FIRST DIVISION SAYS JACK. ROVERS MAKE SHOCK £400,000 BID FOR LUCKLESS STRIKER

122

Sammy signed in time to play in the local derby.

Well, I reckon Pete Ross must be out of his tiny mind! Rovers are facing relegation and he pays a fortune for a striker who can't score!

I just don't understand Sammy Todd. I saw him crack three in for Barton Athletic last season. He was brilliant!

It's like Lester Jack says, he's just not 1st Division material! And now we're stuck with him!

Not expecting a goal-rush from Rovers then, eh, Boss?

With that legless wonder Sammy Todd on their side? Do me a favour, Walt!

From the kick-off, City swept into the attack.

Up the City! Let's have a dozen, lads!

YE-E-ESSSS!

And then, Rovers hit back . . .

You're away on your own, Sammy!

Hit it, Sammy! Now, lad!

I've just got to make this one count!

OOOOOOH!

Oh, no!

Then just on half time.

NOOOOO!

At half-time . . .

Sorry, Boss.

Don't worry, son. You were in the right place both times. Your positional play is first class. Keep it up. The goals will come.

Second half . . .

The boss has got faith in me! I've got to prove him right!

I made it!

YE-E-SSSSS!

I was right, Ernie.

About what, Boss?

The End

Jimmy's Star Choice

LINFORD CHRISTIE

Explosive speed and a tremendous will-to-win have put Linford Christie in the top flight of sprinters. His combination of power and pace has burned up tracks all over the world and made him an opponent to be feared. In one of athletics' most demanding events, where split seconds can make the difference between victory and defeat, lightning-fast Linford has shown he can battle with the best.